African economy
A sleeping giant

By

Roshdy Ebrahim, Ph.D

2020

African economy, a sleeping giant

Copyright © 2020 Roshdy Ebrahim

All right reserved

ISBN: 9798570662773

Contents

Chapter 1 African traditional knowledge to make progress 3

Chapter 2 three ways to uproot a culture of corruption 13

Chapter 3 No aid for Africa 20

Chapter 4 Africa's cheetahs versus hippos 33

Chapter 5 macro finance in Africa 44

Chapter 6 The age-old sharing economies of Africa 48

Chapter 7 Why invest in Africa 55

Chapter 8 Invest in Africa 70

Chapter 9 A vehicle built in Africa, for Africa 82

Chapter 10 Affordable and sustainable electricity in Africa 90

Chapter 11 Energy Africa between developing and fighting climate change 101

Chapter 12 Crop insurance 107

Chapter 13 Farming in Africa 115

References 127

Chapter 1 African traditional knowledge to make progress [1]

Some months back, I was visiting this East African city, and we were stuck in traffic. And this vendor suddenly approaches my window with a half-opened alphabet sheet. I took a quick look at the alphabet sheet, and I thought of my daughter, how it would be nice to spread it on the floor and just play all over it with her while getting her to learn the alphabet. So, the traffic moved a bit, and I quickly grabbed a copy, and we moved on.

When I had time to fully open the alphabet sheet and take a more detailed look at it, I knew I was not going to use that to teach my daughter. I regretted my purchase. Why so? Looking at the alphabet sheet reminded me of the fact that not much has changed in the education curricula in Africa. Some decades back, I was taught out of a similar alphabet sheet. And because of that, I struggled for years. I struggled to reconcile my reality with the formal education I received in

---

)[1] Chika Ezeanya: Before We Set Sail, amazon– March 7, 2012

school, in the schools I attended. I had identity crises. I looked down on my reality. I looked at my ancestry, I looked at my lineage with disrespect. I had very little patience for what my life had to offer around me.

Why? "A is for apple." "A is for apple." "A is for apple" is for that child in that part of the world where apples grow out; who has an apple in her lunch bag; who goes to the grocery store with her mom and sees red, green, yellow -- apples of all shapes and colors and sizes. And so, introducing education to this child with an alphabet sheet like this fulfills one of the major functions of education, which is to introduce the learner to an appreciation of the learner's environment and a curiosity to explore more in order to add value.

In my own case, when and where I grew up in Africa, apple was an exotic fruit. Two or three times a year, I could get some yellowish apples with brown dots, you know, signifying thousands of miles traveled -- warehouses storing -- to get to me. I grew up in the city to very financially comfortable parents, so it was my dignified reality, exactly the same way cassava fufu or ugali would not regularly feature in an American, Chinese or Indian diet, apples didn't count as part of my reality. So, what this did to me, introducing education to me with "A is for apple," made education an abstraction. It made it something out of my reach -- a foreign concept, a phenomenon for which I would have to constantly and perpetually seek the validation of those it belonged to for me to make progress within it and with it. That was tough for a child; it would be tough for anyone.

As I grew up and I advanced academically, my reality was further separated from my education. In history, I was taught that the Scottish explorer Mungo Park discovered the Niger River. And so, it bothered me. My great-great-grandparents grew up quite close to the edge of the Niger River.

And it took someone to travel thousands of miles from Europe to discover a river right under their nose? What did they do with their time?

Playing board games, roasting fresh yams, fighting tribal wars? I mean, I just knew my education was preparing me to go somewhere else and practice and give to another environment that it belonged to. It was not for my environment, where and when I grew up.

And this continued. This philosophy undergirded my studies all through the time I studied in Africa. It took a lot of experiences and some studies for me to begin to have a change of mindset. I will share a couple of the remarkable ones with us.

I was in the United States in Washington, DC studying towards my doctorate, and I got this consultancy position with the World Bank Africa Region. And so, I remember one day, my boss -- we were having a conversation on some project, and he mentioned a particular World Bank project, a large-scale irrigation project that cost millions of dollars in Niger Republic that was faltering sustainably. He said this project wasn't so sustainable, and it bothered those that instituted the whole package. But then he mentioned a particular project, a particular traditional irrigation method that was hugely successful in the same Niger

Republic where the World Bank project was failing. And that got me thinking. So, I did further research, and I found out about Tassa.

Tassa is a traditional irrigation method where 20- to 30-centimeter-wide and 20- to 30-centimeter-deep holes are dug across a field to be cultivated. Then, a small dam is constructed around the field, and then crops are planted across the surface area. What happens is that when rain falls, the holes are able to store the water and appropriate it to the extent that the plant needs the water. The plant can only assimilate as much water as needed until harvest time. Niger is 75 percent scorched desert, so this is something that is a life-or-death situation, and it has been used for centuries. In an experiment that was conducted, two similar plots of land were used in the experiment, and one plot of land did not have the Tassa technique on it. Similar plots. The other one had Tassa technique constructed on it. Then similar grains of millet also were planted on both plots. During harvest time, the plot of land without Tassa technique yielded 11 kilograms of millet per hectare. The plot of land with Tassa technique yielded 553 kilograms of millet per hectare.

I looked at the research, and I looked at myself. I said, "I studied agriculture for 12 years, from primary to Senior Six, as we say in East Africa, SS3 in West Africa or 12th grade. No one ever taught me of any form of traditional African knowledge of cultivation -- of harvesting, of anything -- that will work in modern times and actually succeed, where something imported from the West would struggle to succeed. That was when I knew the challenge, the challenge of Africa's curricula, And I thus began my quest to dedicate my life, concern my life work, to studying, conducting research on Africa's own knowledge system and being able to advocate for its mainstreaming in education, in research, policy across sectors and industries.

Another conversation and experience I had at the bank I guess made me take that final decision of where I was going to go, even though it wasn't the most lucrative research to go into, but it was just about what I believed in. And so, one day, my boss said that he likes to go to Africa to negotiate World Bank loans and to work on World Bank projects. And I was intrigued. I asked him why. He said, "Oh, when I go to Africa, it's so easy. I just write up my loan documents and my project proposal in Washington, DC, I go to Africa, and they all just get signed. I get the best deal, and I'm back to base. My bosses are happy with me."

But then he said, "I hate going to Asia or ..." and he mentioned a particular country, Asia and some of these countries. "They keep me for this, trying to get the best deal for their countries. They get the best deal. They tell me, 'Oh, that clause will not work for us in our environment. It's not our reality. It's just so Western.' And they tell me, 'Oh, we have enough experts to take care of this. You don't have enough experts. We know our aim.' And they just keep going through all these things. By the time they finish, yes, they get the best deal, but I'm so exhausted and I don't get the best deal for the bank, and we're in business." "Really?" I thought in my head, "OK."

I was privileged to sit in on a loan negotiating session in an African country. So I would do these consultancy positions during summer, you know, since I was a doctoral student. And then I traveled with the team, with the World Bank team, as more like someone to help out with organizational matters. But I sat in during the negotiating session. I had mostly Euro-Americans, you know, with me from Washington, DC. And I looked across the table at my African brothers and sisters. I could see intimidation on their faces. They didn't believe they had anything to offer the great-great-grandchildren of Mungo Park -- the owners of "apple" in "A is for apple." They just sat and watched: "Oh, just give us, let us sign. You own the knowledge. You know it all. Just, where do we sign? Show us, let us sign." They had no voice. They didn't believe in themselves.

I have been conducting research on Africa's knowledge system, original, authentic, traditional knowledge. In the few cases where this has been implemented in Africa, there has been remarkable successes recorded.

I think of Gacaca. Gacaca is Rwanda's traditional judicial system that was used after the genocide. In 1994, when the genocide ended, Rwanda's national court system was in shambles: no judges, no lawyers to try hundreds of thousands of genocide cases. So, the government of Rwanda came up with this idea to resuscitate a traditional judicial system known as Gacaca. Gacaca is a community-based judicial system, where community members come together to elect men and women of proven integrity to try cases of crimes committed within these communities. So, by the time Gacaca concluded its trial of genocide cases in 2012, 12,000 community-based courts had tried approximately 1.2 million cases. That's a record.

Most importantly is that Gacaca emphasized Rwanda's traditional philosophy of reconciliation and reintegration, as against the whole punitive and banishment idea that undergirds present-day Western style. And not to compare, but just to say that it really emphasized Rwanda's traditional method of philosophy.

And so, it was Mwalimu Julius Nyerere, former president of Tanzania who said that you cannot develop people. People will have to develop themselves. I agree with Mwalimu. I am convinced that Africa's further transformation, Africa's advancement, rests simply in the acknowledgment, validation and mainstreaming of Africa's own traditional, authentic, original, indigenous knowledge in education, in research, in policy making and across sectors. This is not going to be easy for Africa. It is not going to be easy for a people used to being told how to think, what to do, how to go about it, a people long subjected to the intellectual guidance and direction of others, be they the colonial masters, aid industry or international news media. But it is a task that we have to do to make progress.

I am strengthened by the words of Joseph Shabalala, founder of the South African choral group Ladysmith Black Mambazo. He said that the task ahead of us can never, ever be greater than the power within us. We can do it. We can unlearn looking down on ourselves. We can learn to place value on our reality and our knowledge.

Chapter 2 three ways to uproot a culture of corruption [1]

Have you ever been robbed? Or had something you value forcibly taken from you against your will? It's violating. Feelings of fury, of assault and of helplessness. That's what corruption feels like. Corruption is theft. It is corrosive, it is criminal, it is toxic and it is predatory.

Now, I'm from Kenya, and in Kenya, corruption takes different forms. I want to share the story of Karura Forest with you. This is my hometown of Nairobi. I love Nairobi. It's beautiful. But it is a city of paradoxes. It is at once beautiful and challenging. But at the heart of this beautiful city that I call home is Karura Forest, an oasis of green, expansive beauty that would be the envy of any city anywhere. We almost lost Karura Forest to corruption. Word has reached my mother, Wangari Maathai, that Karura Forest is under attack. There was a construction site coming up

---

[1] Wanjira Mathai: environmentalist, social entrepreneur, youth leadership advocate.

right in the middle of the forest. Government officials had stolen the forest. They had divided, sold and gifted hundreds of parcels of Karura to their friends and cronies.

Now in 1977, my mother founded the Green Belt Movement to plant trees across Kenya, restore green spaces and protect green spaces, much like Karura Forest. She got together her friends and allies, and together, they created what became one of the most successful tree-planting campaigns in the world. It was therefore no surprise that when word got to her that Karura was under attack, they immediately sprang into action. They battled police and hired goons to stop the theft of this forest. But fortunately, there was an uprising of support from the clergy, politicians, students and the general public, all of whom came out to say no to corruption and greed. And pretty soon, that support was too strong and intense for the authorities to subdue. And Karura Forest was saved.

In the 2000s, I joined my mother in the Green Belt Movement and witnessed the growth of the movement's advocacy activities, its expansion beyond Kenya and an extremely important growing consensus around the 2004 Nobel Peace Prize that she received -- that the environment, democracy and peace were inextricably linked. I also learned that what my mother had faced that many years ago trying to protect Karura Forest was not an isolated incident. The corruption and greed that manifested itself then is alive and well today, from greedy politicians and public servants willing to loot public coffers at their expense.

Corruption is everywhere. Now, corruption is devastating to any economy, democracy and the environment. It robs citizens of vital social services and renders human life worthless. When young men are willing to join gangs and brutalize their communities for a small fee, and women are raped on the way to work, and, when they report this, the perpetrators bribe their way out of jail, and when young girls have to sell their bodies to buy sanitary towels, you know the society is broken.

In recent years, Kenya has been ranked amongst the top 10 most corrupt countries in the world. Even more frustrating for me is that Kenya loses a third of her national budget to corruption each year. That is six billion dollars. It is totally unacceptable. In a country where anti-corruption efforts have been frustrated and ignored and interfered with, we absolutely need new strategies for dealing with this vice. We cannot complain forever. We either decide that we're going to live with it or we are going to change it.

There's some good news. Human beings are not born corrupt. At some point, these behaviors are fostered by a culture that promotes individual gain over collective progress. So, if we're going to uproot corruption, we have got to start before it ever takes root. We have got to intervene early. I don't know about your country, but where I come from, youth will lead us into the future.

In Kenya today, 80 percent of the population is under the age of 35. But by their own admission, they have conflicting values. Fifty-eight percent of young people in Kenya recently told us they will do anything to make money. An additional 45 percent said corruption is a legitimate tool for doing business. Seventy-three percent said they would not be willing to stand up for what they believe in for fear of retribution.

What I learned from my mother a few years ago was this concept of "the power of one" -- that each of us can be potent agents of change and that together, we are a force, that if we put our hands together, we can change the situation and no problem is too big. My mother understood this so profoundly that it was at the center of her work. Shifting cultures takes patience, persistence and commitment, and it is extremely slow and deep work. But if we are going to shift a culture, we have got to get that work started. And in the time since her passing, we have established a foundation in her name to do exactly that but to work with young people and children to begin to build character and personal leadership, to inspire purpose and integrity. But fighting corruption is not as easy as saying corruption is bad.

Now, here are three strategies that we are employing that we believe can be replicated in any school community. First, we must understand the why: Why does corruption happen in the first place? Do we call it for what it is -- theft -- or do we gloss over it with other words? When young children are able to model what it looks and feels like to deal with corruption, they are likely, when faced with a dilemma in their future, to model what they've been taught.

Second, we need to teach character explicitly. Now, this may seem obvious, but a child who exhibits a growth mindset and a sense of self-control is self-confident. And a self-confident child is likely to stand up for what they believe.

Third, we need to build personal leadership in our children early to give them an opportunity to know what it looks like to call corruption out when they see it, what it feels like to stand up and be counted when they're needed and, for me, to make the more and most important connection between human suffering on one hand and corruption, greed and selfishness on the other.

We have got to believe in our capacity to bring about the future we want to see, each of us in our small way. Young people must believe that a new reality is possible. Corruption, climate change, ecosystem collapse, biodiversity loss -- all these issues need leadership.

And in the words of Baba Dioum of Senegal, "In the final analysis, we will conserve only what we love, we will love only what we understand and we will understand only what we are taught."

Chapter 3 No aid for Africa [1]

We are hosting this conference at a very opportune moment, because another conference is taking place in Berlin. It is the G8 Summit. The G8 Summit proposes that the solution to Africa's problems should be a massive increase in aid, something akin to the Marshall Plan. Unfortunately, I personally do not believe in the Marshall Plan. One, because the benefits of the Marshall Plan have been overstated. Its largest recipients were Germany and France, and it was only 2.5 percent of their GDP. An average African country receives foreign aid to the tune of 13, 15 percent of its GDP, and that is an unprecedented transfer of financial resources from rich countries to poor countries.

But I want to say that there are two things we need to connect. How the media covers Africa in the West, and the consequences of that. By displaying despair, helplessness and hopelessness, the media is telling the truth about Africa, and nothing but the truth. However, the

---

)[1] Andrew Mwenda: journalist

media is not telling us the whole truth. Because despair, civil war, hunger and famine, although they're part and parcel of our African reality, they are not the only reality. And secondly, they are the smallest reality.

Africa has 53 nations. We have civil wars only in six countries, which means that the media are covering only six countries. Africa has immense opportunities that never navigate through the web of despair and helplessness that the Western media largely presents to its audience. But the effect of that presentation is, it appeals to sympathy. It appeals to pity. It appeals to something called charity. And, as a consequence, the Western view of Africa's economic dilemma is framed wrongly. The wrong framing is a product of thinking that Africa is a place of despair. What should we do with it? We should give food to the hungry. We should deliver medicines to those who are ill. We should send peacekeeping troops to serve those who are facing a civil war. And in the process, Africa has been stripped of self-initiative.

I want to say that it is important to recognize that Africa has fundamental weaknesses. But equally, it has opportunities and a lot of potential. We need to reframe the challenge that is facing Africa, from a challenge of despair, which is called poverty reduction, to a challenge of hope. We frame it as a challenge of hope, and that is worth creation. The challenge facing all those who are interested in Africa is not the challenge of reducing poverty. It should be a challenge of creating wealth.

Once we change those two things -- if you say the Africans are poor and they need poverty reduction, you have the international cartel of good intentions moving onto the continent, with what? Medicines for the poor, food relief for those who are hungry, and peacekeepers for those who are facing civil war. And in the process, none of these things really are productive because you are treating the symptoms, not the causes of Africa's fundamental problems. Sending somebody to school and giving them medicines, ladies and gentlemen, does not create wealth for them. Wealth is a function of income, and income comes from you finding a profitable trading opportunity or a well-paying job.

Now, once we begin to talk about wealth creation in Africa, our second challenge will be, who are the wealth-creating agents in any society? They are entrepreneurs. they are always about four percent of the population, but 16 percent are imitators. But they also succeed at the job of entrepreneurship. So, where should we be putting the money? We need to put money where it can productively grow. Support private investment in Africa, both domestic and foreign. Support research institutions, because knowledge is an important part of wealth creation.

But what is the international aid community doing with Africa today? They are throwing large sums of money for primary health, for primary education, for food relief. The entire continent has been turned into a place of despair, in need of charity. Ladies and gentlemen, can any one of you tell me a neighbor, a friend, a relative that you know, who became rich by receiving charity? By holding the begging bowl and receiving alms? Does any one of you in the audience have that person? Does any one of you know a country that developed because of the generosity and kindness of another? Well, since I'm not seeing the hand, it appears that what I'm stating is true.

But let me tell you this. External actors can only present to you an opportunity. The ability to utilize that opportunity and turn it into an advantage depends on your internal capacity. Africa has received many opportunities. Many of them we haven't benefited much. Why? Because we lack the internal, institutional framework and policy framework that can make it possible for us to benefit from our external relations. I'll give you an example.

Under the Cotonou Agreement, formerly known as the Lome Convention, African countries have been given an opportunity by Europe to export goods, duty-free, to the European Union market. My own country, Uganda, has a quota to export 50,000 metric tons of sugar to the European Union market. We haven't exported one kilogram yet. We import 50,000 metric tons of sugar from Brazil and Cuba. Secondly, under the beef protocol of that agreement, African countries that produce beef have quotas to export beef duty-free to the European Union market. None of those countries, including Africa's most successful nation, Botswana, has ever met its quota.

So, I want to argue today that the fundamental source of Africa's inability to engage the rest of the world in a more productive relationship is because it has a poor institutional and policy framework. And all forms of intervention need support, the evolution of the kinds of institutions that create wealth, the kinds of institutions that increase productivity. How do we begin to do that, and why is aid the bad instrument? Aid is the bad instrument, and do you know why? Because all governments across the world need money to survive. Money is needed for a simple thing like keeping law and order. You have to pay the army and the police to show law and order. And because many of our governments are quite dictatorial, they need really to have the army clobber the opposition. The second thing you need to do is pay your political hangers-on. Why should people support their government? Well, because it gives them good, paying jobs, or, in many African countries, unofficial opportunities to profit from corruption.

The fact is no government in the world, with the exception of a few, like that of Idi Amin, can seek to depend entirely on force as an instrument of rule. Many countries in the [unclear], they need legitimacy. To get legitimacy, governments often need to deliver things like primary education, primary health, roads, build hospitals and clinics. If the government's fiscal survival depends on it having to raise money from its own people, such a government is driven by self-interest to govern in a more enlightened fashion. It will sit with those who create wealth. Talk to them about the kind of policies and institutions that are necessary for them to expand a scale and scope of business so that it can collect more tax revenues from them. The problem with the African continent and the problem with the aid industry is that it has distorted the structure of incentives facing the governments in Africa. The productive margin in our governments' search for revenue does not lie in the domestic economy, it lies with international donors.

rather than sit with Ugandan entrepreneurs, Ghanaian businessmen, South African enterprising leaders, our governments find it more productive to talk to the IMF and the World Bank. I can tell you, even if you have ten Ph.Ds., you can never beat Bill Gates in understanding the computer industry. Why? Because the knowledge that is required for you to understand the incentives necessary to expand a business -- it requires that you listen to the people, the private sector actors in that industry.

Governments in Africa have therefore been given an opportunity, by the international community, to avoid building productive arrangements with your own citizens, and therefore allowed to begin endless negotiations with the IMF and the World Bank, and then it is the IMF and the World Bank that tell them what its citizens need. In the process, we, the African people, have been sidelined from the policy-making, policy-orientation, and policy- implementation process in our countries. We have limited input, because he who pays the piper calls the tune. The IMF, the World Bank, and the cartel of good intentions in the world has taken over our rights as citizens, and therefore what our governments are doing, because they depend on aid, is to listen to international creditors rather than their own citizens.

But I want to put a caveat on my argument, and that caveat is that it is not true that aid is always destructive. Some aid may have built a hospital, fed a hungry village. It may have built a road, and that road may have served a very good role. The mistake of the international aid industry is to pick these isolated incidents of success, generalize them, pour billions and trillions of dollars into them, and then spread them across the whole world, ignoring the specific and unique circumstances in a given village, the skills, the practices, the norms and habits that allowed that small aid project to succeed -- like in Sauri village, in Kenya, where Jeffrey Sachs is working -- and therefore generalize this experience as the experience of everybody.

Aid increases the resources available to governments, and that makes working in a government the most profitable thing you can have, as a person in Africa seeking a career. By increasing the political attractiveness of the state, especially in our ethnically fragmented societies in Africa, aid tends to accentuate ethnic tensions as every single ethnic group now begins struggling to enter the state in order to get access to the foreign aid pie. Ladies and gentlemen, the most enterprising people in Africa cannot find opportunities to trade and to work in the private sector because the institutional and policy environment is hostile to business. Governments are not changing it. Why? Because they don't need to talk to their own citizens. They talk to international donors. So, the most enterprising Africans end up going to work for government, and that has increased the political tensions in our countries precisely because we depend on aid.

I also want to say that it is important for us to note that, over the last 50 years, Africa has been receiving increasing aid from the international community, in the form of technical assistance, and financial aid, and all other forms of aid. Between 1960 and 2003, our continent received 600 billion dollars of aid, and we are still told that there is a lot of poverty in Africa. Where has all the aid gone?

I want to use the example of my own country, called Uganda, and the kind of structure of incentives that aid has brought there. In the 2006-2007 budget, expected revenue: 2.5 trillion shillings. The expected foreign aid: 1.9 trillion. Uganda's recurrent expenditure -- by recurrent what do I mean? Hand-to-mouth is 2.6 trillion. Why does the government of Uganda budget spend 110 percent of its own revenue? It's because there's somebody there called foreign aid, who contributes for it. But this shows you that the government of Uganda is not committed to spending its own revenue to invest in productive investments, but rather it devotes this revenue to paying structure of public expenditure. Public administration, which is largely patronage, takes 690 billion. The military, 380 billion. Agriculture, which employs 18 percent of our poverty-stricken citizens, takes only 18 billion. Trade and industry take 43 billion. And let me show you, what does public expenditure -- rather, public administration expenditure -- in Uganda constitute? There you go. 70 cabinet ministers, 114 presidential advisers, by the way, who never see the president, except on television.

And when they see him physically, it is at public functions like this, and even there, it is him who advises them.

We have 81 units of local government. Each local government is organized like the central government -- a bureaucracy, a cabinet, a parliament, and so many jobs for the political hangers-on. There were 56, and when our president wanted to amend the constitution and remove term limits, he had to create 25 new districts, and now there are 81. Three hundred thirty-three members of parliament. You need Wembley Stadium to host our parliament. One hundred thirty-four commissions and semi-autonomous government bodies, all of which have directors and the cars.

A recent government of Uganda study found that there are 3,000 four-wheel drive motor vehicles at the Minister of Health headquarters. Uganda has 961 sub-counties, each of them with a dispensary, none of which has an ambulance. So, the four-wheel drive vehicles at the headquarters drive the ministers, the permanent secretaries, the bureaucrats and the international aid bureaucrats who work in aid projects, while the poor die without ambulances and medicine.

Chapter 4 Africa's cheetahs versus hippos [1]

The Cheetah Generation is a new breed of Africans who brook no nonsense about corruption. They understand what accountability and democracy is. They're not going to wait for government to do things for them. That's the Cheetah Generation, and Africa's salvation rests on the backs of these Cheetahs. In contrast, of course, we have the Hippo Generation.

The Hippo Generation are the ruling elites. They are stuck in their intellectual patch. Complaining about colonialism and imperialism, they wouldn't move one foot. If you ask them to reform the economies, they're not going to reform it because they benefit from the rotten status quo. Now, there are a lot of Africans who are very angry, angry at the condition of Africa. Now, we're talking about a continent that is not poor. It is rich in mineral resources, natural mineral resources. But the mineral wealth of Africa is not being utilized to lift its people out of poverty. That's

---

)[1] G. Ayitta: Africa Unchained: The Blueprint for Africa's Future, amazon 2006

what makes a lot of Africans very angry. And in a way, Africa is more than a tragedy, in more ways than one. There's another enduring tragedy, and that tragedy is that there are so many people, so many governments, so many organizations who want to help the people in Africa. They don't understand. Now, we're not saying don't help Africa. Helping Africa is noble. But helping Africa has been turned into a theater of the absurd. It's like the blind leading the clueless.

There are certain things that we need to recognize. Africa's begging-bowl leaks. Did you know that 40 percent of the wealth created in Africa is not invested here in Africa? It's taken out of Africa. That's what the World Bank says. Look at Africa's begging-bowl. It leaks horribly. There are people who think that we should pour more money, more aid into this bowl which leaks. What are the leakages? Corruption alone costs Africa 148 billion dollars a year. Yes, put that aside. Capital flight out of Africa, 80 billion a year. Put that aside. Let's take food imports. Every year Africa spends 20 billion dollars to import food. Just add that up, all these leakages. That's far more than the

50 billion Tony Blair wants to raise for Africa. Now, back in the 1960s Africa not only fed itself, it also exported food. Not anymore.

We know that something has gone fundamentally wrong. You know it, I know it, but let's not waste our time talking about these mistakes because we'll spend all day here. Let's move on, and flip over to the next chapter. The next chapter begins with first of all, asking ourselves this fundamental question, "Whom do we want to help in Africa?" There are the people, and then there is the government or leaders. Now, the previous speaker before me, Idris Mohammed, indicated that we've had abysmal leadership in Africa. That characterization, in my view, is even more charitable.

I belong to an Internet discussion forum, an African Internet discussion forum, and I asked them, I said, "Since 1960, we've had exactly 204 African heads of state, since 1960." And I asked them to name me just 20 good leaders, just 20 good leaders -- you may want to take this leadership challenge yourself. I asked them to name me just

20. Everybody mentioned Nelson Mandela, of course. Kwame Nkrumah, Nyerere, Kenyatta -- somebody mentioned Idi Amin.

My point is, they couldn't go beyond 15. Even if they had been able to name me 20, what does that tell you? 20 out of 204 means that the vast majority of the African leaders failed their people. And if you look at them, the slate of the post-colonial leaders -- an assortment of military fufu heads, Swiss-bank socialists, crocodile liberators, vampire elites, quack revolutionaries.

Now, this leadership is a far cry from the traditional leaders that Africans have known for centuries. The second false premise that we make when we're trying to help Africa is that sometimes we think that there is something called a government in Africa that cares about its people, serves the interests of the people, and represents the people. There is one particular quote -- a Lesotho chief once said that "Here in Lesotho, we've got two problems: rats and the government."

What you and I understand as a government doesn't exist in many African countries. In fact, what we call our governments are vampire states. Vampires because they suck the economic vitality out of their people. Government is the problem in Africa. A vampire state is the government -- (Applause) -- which has been hijacked by a phalanx of bandits and crooks who use the instruments of state power to enrich themselves, their cronies, and tribesmen and exclude everybody else. The richest people in Africa are heads-of-state and ministers, and quite often the chief bandit is the head-of-state himself. Where do they get their money? By creating wealth? No. By raking it off the backs of their suffering people. That's not wealth creation. It's wealth redistribution.

The third fundamental issue that we have to recognize is that if we want to help the African people, we must know where the African people are. Take any African economy. An African economy can be broken up into three sectors. There is the modern sector, there is the informal sector and the traditional sector. The modern sector is the abode of the elites. It's the seat of government. In many African countries the modern sector is lost. It's dysfunctional. It is a meretricious fandango of imported systems, which the elites themselves don't understand. That is the source of many of Africa's problems where the struggles for political power emanate and then spill over onto the informal and the traditional sector, claiming innocent lives.

Now the modern sector, of course, is where a lot of the development aid and resources went into. More than 80 percent of Ivory Coast's development went into the modern sector. The other sectors, the informal and the traditional sectors, are where you find the majority of the African people, the real people in Africa. That's where you find them. Now, obviously it makes common sense that if you want to help the people, you go where the people are. But that's not what we did. As a matter of fact, we neglected the informal and the traditional sectors. Now, traditional sector is where Africa produces its agriculture, which is one of the reasons why Africa can't feed itself, and that's why it must import food.

All right, you cannot develop Africa by ignoring the informal and the traditional sectors. And you can't develop the informal and the traditional sectors without an operational understanding of how these two sectors work. These two sectors, let me describe to you, have their own indigenous institutions. First one is the political system. Traditionally, Africans hate governments. They hate tyranny. If you look into their traditional systems, Africans organize their states in two types. The first one belongs to those ethnic societies who believe that the state was necessarily tyrannous, so they didn't want to have anything to do with any centralized authority. These societies are the Ibo, the Somali, the Kikuyus, for example. They have no chiefs.

The other ethnic groups, which did have chiefs, made sure that they surrounded the chiefs with councils upon councils upon councils to prevent them from abusing their power. In Ashanti tradition, for example, the chief cannot make any decision without the concurrence of the council of elders. Without the council the chief can't pass any law, and if the chief doesn't govern according to the will of the people he will be removed. If not, the people will abandon the chief, go somewhere else and set up a new settlement. And even if you look in ancient African empires, they were all organized around one particular principle -- the confederacy principle, which is characterized by a great deal of devolution of authority, decentralization of power.

Now, this is what I have described to you. This is part of Africa's indigenous political heritage. Now, compare that to the modern systems the ruling elites established on Africa. It is a total far cry. In the economic system in traditional Africa, the means of production is privately owned. It's owned by extended families. You see, in the West, the basic economic and social unit is the individual. The American will say, "I am because I am, and I can damn well do anything I want, anytime." The accent is on the "I." In Africa, the Africans say, "I am, because we are." The "we" connotes community -- the extended family system. The extended family system pools its resources together.

They own farms. They decide what to do, what to produce. They don't take any orders from their chiefs. They decide what to do. And when they produce their crops, they sell the surplus on marketplaces. When they make a profit, it is theirs to keep, not for the chief to sequester it from them. So, in a nutshell, what we had in traditional Africa was a free-market system. There were markets in Africa before the colonialists stepped foot on the continent. Timbuktu was one great big market town. Kano, Salaga -- they were all there. Even if you go to West Africa, you notice that market activity in West Africa has always been dominated by women. So, it's quite appropriate that this section is called a marketplace. The market is not alien to Africa.

What Africans practiced was a different form of capitalism, but then after independence, all of a sudden, markets, capitalism became a western institution, and the leaders said Africans were ready for socialism. Nonsense. And even then, what kind of socialism did they practice? The socialism that they practiced was a peculiar form of Swiss-bank socialism, which allowed the heads of states and the ministers to rape and plunder Africa's treasuries for deposit in Switzerland. That is not the kind of system Africans had known for centuries. What do we do now? Go back to Africa's indigenous institutions, and this is where we charge the Cheetahs to go into the informal sectors, the traditional sectors. That's where you find the African people.

And I'd like to show you a quick little video about the informal sector, about the boat-building that I, myself, tried to mobilize Africans in the Diaspora to invest in. Could you please show that? The men are going fishing in these small boats. Yes, it's an enterprise. This is by a local Ghanaian entrepreneur, using his own capital. He's getting no assistance from the government, and he's building a second, bigger boat. A bigger boat will mean more fish will be caught and landed. It means that he will be able to employ more Ghanaians. It also means that he will be able to generate wealth. And then it will have what economists call external effects on a local economy. All that you need to do, all that the elites need to do, is to move this operation into something that is enclosed so that the operation can be made more efficient.

Now, it is not just this informal sector. There is also traditional medicine. 80 percent of Africans still rely on traditional medicine. The modern healthcare sector has totally collapsed. Now, this is an area -- I mean, there is a treasure trove of wealth in the traditional medicine area. This is where we need to mobilize Africans, in the Diaspora especially, to invest in this. We also need to mobilize Africans in the Diaspora, not only to go into the traditional sectors, but to go into agriculture and also to instigate change from within. We were able to mobilize Ghanaians in the Diaspora to instigate change in Ghana and bring about democracy in Ghana. And I know that with the Cheetahs, we can take Africa back one village at a time.

Chapter 5 macro finance in Africa [1]

Traditional prescriptions for growth in Africa are not working very well. After one trillion dollars in African development-related aid in the last 60 years, real per capita income today is lower than it was in the 1970s. Aid is not doing too well.

In response, the Bretton Woods institutions -- the IMF and the World Bank -- pushed for free trade not aid, yet the historical record shows little empirical evidence that free trade leads to economic growth.

The newly prescribed silver bullet is microcredit. We seem to be fixated on this romanticized idea that every poor peasant in Africa is an entrepreneur. Yet my work and travel in 40-plus countries across Africa have taught me that most people want jobs instead.

My solution: Forget micro-entrepreneurs. Let's invest in building pan-African titans like Sudanese businessman Mo Ibrahim. Mo took a contrarian bet on Africa when he founded

---

[1] Sangu Delle: entrepreneur and clean water activist.

Celtel International in '98 and built it into a mobile cellular provider with 24 million subscribers across 14 African countries by 2004. The Mo model might be better than the everyman entrepreneur model, which prevents an effective means of diffusion and knowledge-sharing. Perhaps we are not at a stage in Africa where many actors and small enterprises leads to growth through competition.

Consider these two alternative scenarios. One: You loan 200 dollars to each of 500 banana farmers allowing them to dry their surplus bananas and fetch 15 percent more revenue at the local market. Or two: You give 100,000 dollars to one savvy entrepreneur and help her set up a factory that yields 40 percent additional income to all 500 banana farmers and creates 50 additional jobs. We invested in the second scenario, and backed 26-year-old Kenyan entrepreneur Eric Muthomi to set up an agro-processing factory called Stawi to produce gluten-free banana-based flour and baby food. Stawi is leveraging economies of scale and using modern manufacturing processes to create value for not only its owners but its workers, who have an ownership in the business. Our dream is to take an Eric Muthomi and try to help him become a Mo Ibrahim, which requires skill, financing, local and global partnerships, and extraordinary perseverance.

But why pan-African? The scramble for Africa during the Berlin Conference of 1884 -- where, quite frankly, we Africans were not exactly consulted in massive fragmentation and many sovereign states with small populations: Liberia, four million; Cape Verde, 500,000. Pan-Africa gives you one billion people, granted across 55 countries with trade barriers and other impediments, but our ancestors traded across the continent before Europeans drew lines around us. The pan-African opportunities outweigh the challenges, and that's why we're expanding Stawi's markets from just Kenya to Algeria, Nigeria, Ghana, and anywhere else that will buy our food. We hope to help solve food security, empower farmers, create jobs, develop the local economy, and we hope to become rich in the process. While it's not the sexiest approach, and maybe it doesn't achieve the same feel-good as giving a woman 100 dollars to buy a goat on kiva.org, perhaps supporting fewer, higher-impact entrepreneurs to build massive businesses that scale pan-Africa can help change this.

The political freedom for which our forebearers fought is meaningless without economic freedom. We hope to aid this fight for economic freedom by building world-class businesses, creating indigenous wealth, providing jobs that we so desperately need, and hopefully helping achieve this.

I think there is a role. Microcredit has been a great, innovative way to expand financial access to the bottom of the pyramid. But for the problems we face in Africa, when we are looking at the Marshall Plan to revitalize war-torn Europe, it was not full of donations of sheep. We need more than just microcredit. We need more than just give 200 dollars. We need to build big businesses, and we need jobs.

Chapter 6 The age-old sharing economies of Africa [1]

So, what I'm doing is a thought experiment. Now you may know of or have read this book by this guy. It's probably the first and maybe the only bestseller ever written about economics. And you probably know a bit about what it says. It talks about how nations all over the world will prosper through the individual pursuit of individual profit. Individual profit will be the mechanism for the prosperity of the world. But the funny thing about Adam Smith is that he was a stay-at-home kind of guy. He actually never went further from Edinburgh than France and Switzerland. So, my thought experiment is to imagine what would have happened if Adam Smith had visited Africa.

And fortunately, there's actually an easy answer, because the Arab lawyer and traveler Ibn Battuta traveled down the east coast of Africa in the 14th century, and what he found when he got to Mogadishu was a market, and he wrote about

---

[1] Robert Neuwirth: author

it. And basically, merchant ships came to the harbor, and they weren't even allowed to land. They had to drop anchor in the harbor, and boats came out to them, and locals picked them and said, "You are my guest, I am now your broker." And they had to do business through the local broker, and if they went around that and didn't do business through the broker, they could go to court, and the deal would be canceled, and they would be thrown out of town. And through this mechanism, everyone prospered.

And so, if that was Adam Smith, he might look like this guy and say, "Ah! That's a mutual aid society. That's a share-the-wealth free market." And when I put this question to Christian [Benimana], who had the stage at the beginning of this session, he responded that if Adam Smith had come to Africa, there would have been a sharing economy long before Airbnb and Uber. And that's true. So, if we put this to work today, it would be very interesting. There would be a lot of money flowing into the countries. These are just figuring of 10 percent of exports in these countries.

So, the interesting thing is that this mutual aid economy still exists, and we can find examples of it in the strangest places. So, this is Alaba International Market. It's the largest electronics market in West Africa. It's 10,000 merchants, they do about four billion dollars of turnover every year. And they say they are ardent apostles of Adam Smith: competition is great, we're all in it individually, government doesn't help us. But the interesting reality is that when I asked further, that's not what grew the market at all. There's a behind-the-scenes principle that enables this market to grow. And they do claim -- you know, this is an interesting juxtaposition of the King James Bible and "How to Sell Yourself." That's what they say is their message. But in reality, this market is governed by a sharing principle. Every merchant, when you ask them, "How did you get started in global trade?" they say, "Well, when my master settled me." And when I finally got it into my head to ask, "What is this 'settling?'" it turns out that when you've done your apprenticeship with someone you work for, they are required to set you up in business. That means paying your rent for two or three years and giving you a cash infusion so you can go out in the world and start trading. That's locally generated venture capital. Right? And I can say with almost certainty that the Igbo apprenticeship system that governs Alaba International Market is the largest business incubator platform in the world.

And there are other sharing economies that we look for -- merry-go-rounds, which are found in almost every shantytown. They have different names in other cultures; this is the Kenyan name. It's a way of generating cash. It's a kitty -- people throw money into a pot once a week, and once a week, one member of the group gets the money, and they can spend it on whatever they need to.

And there's also something called "acequias," and that is a Spanish word, but it comes from the North African Arabic; "saqiya" means "water wheel." And what the acequia is a sharing system for scarce water. It's migrated from North Africa to Spain, and from Spain to the west of the United States, where it still is used. And it shares water by need rather than by who was there first. And contrary, with all due respect, to what Llew [Claasen] said when he talked about blockchains and cryptocurrencies yesterday, there is no tragedy of the commons. People in acequias have been commonly managing scarce water resources for hundreds and hundreds and hundreds of years.

So, taking this thought experiment, I wanted to go a little bit further and suggest that these things are managed communally, and they are taking care of scarce capital, scarce cash and scarce resources. And it seems to me that we have actually two kinds of capitalism. We have the capitalism of the top up. And these are really interesting statistics, because three one-thousandths of one percent of the Nigerian population controls wealth equal to one-fourth of the GDP of the country. One one-hundredth of one percent of the Kenyan population controls wealth equal to 75 percent of the GDP of the country. That's the capitalism of top up. And everyone else is with this guy, selling board games and bodybuilding equipment in a go-slow on the highway in Lagos. And when you're selling board games and bodybuilding equipment in a go-slow, that traffic jam is really, really, really bad, right?

Those of us in this sphere of the economy are caught in what I call "the capitalism of decay," because there's no way to rise up and get out of it, because they're lacking the resources that we talked about in those sharing economies. And they're tripped up by the thesis of cassava and capitalism, that cassava has to be processed in order not to be poisonous, and I would argue that, similarly, the market economy needs to be processed in order to be fair to everyone.

So we have to look at what I call the "bottom down economy." These are these sharing models that exist out there that need to be propagated and used and scaled. OK? And if we propagate these things, we can begin to bring infrastructure to everyone, and that will ensure that communities are leading their own development, which is, I believe, what we need in the world, and, I would suggest, what we need in Africa.

I wanted to quote Steve Biko, and I thought it was really important to quote Steve Biko, because next month, September 12 to be exact, is the 40th anniversary of his murder by the South African state. And you can read the quote. He basically said that we're not here to compete. And I love this quote: "... to make us a community of brothers and sisters jointly involved in the quest for a composite answer to the varied problems of life." And he also said that "the great powers of the world have done wonders in giving us an industrial and military look, ..." and we don't have to copy that military-industrialist complex, because Africa can do things differently and restore the humanity of the world.

And so, what I want to suggest here is that we have an opportunity, that we are all here in the mutual landscape to be able to do things, and that the journey starts now.

Chapter 7 Why invest in Africa [1]

Welcome to Africa! Or rather, I should say, welcome home. Because this is where it all really began, isn't it? Looking at fossils dating back several millions of years -- it all points to evidence that life for the human species as we know it began right here. We are on an amazing journey the next four days. You're going to hear stories of "Africa" Fantastic tales, anecdotes. But I want to turn that upside down for a moment, and get something out on the table and clear the air so to say. What's the worst thing you've ever heard about Africa? And this is not a rhetorical question. I actually want answers from you. Go for it! The worst. Famine. Corruption. More. Genocide. AIDS. Slavery. That's enough.

We've all heard these things. But this is about Africa, the story we have not heard. The stories that we want to know, and the stories that do exist about positive tales. A part of my talk is going to be about investment opportunities that exist on this continent, to separate the rhetoric from the

---

)[1] Euvin Naidoo: investment banker

reality, the fact from the fiction. To go to the actual data and statistics that exist about the actual things that are happening on the ground that make Africa a realistic investment opportunity and option for you. So let's get going because Africa, to some degree, is on a turnaround. A turnaround in terms of how it manages its image, and how it takes control of its own destiny. And turnarounds are part and parcel of what I have focused on for most of my professional career. And it all started almost a decade ago, as a young consultant at McKinsey & Company at their first African office in Johannesburg.

And there we worked with leading CEOs on African issues, and African companies on turnarounds, making the companies not just the best in Africa but the best globally. But I really formalized this focus on turnarounds when I was completing my MBA in the United States. It all began with a fantastic phone call. It was from Rosabeth Moss Kanter, Harvard Business School guru and a professor of mine. And she said, "I want to write a case, Euvin -- a case on a public-sector leader that has lessons for the corporate world." And the leader that came to mind was Nelson Mandela. Because Nelson Mandela, as he took over power as the first democratically-elected president of South Africa, faced a situation of a country that could have slid into the abyss of chaos. But he started the country on a path of a positive cycle.

Now the case, "Nelson Mandela: Change Leader," became part of the research base for a chapter in Rosabeth's new book called "Confidence." And "Confidence" became a New York Times bestseller and topped Business Week's hardcover bestseller list. And why I tell you this story is because later, when I was interviewed on SABC Africa, on a pan-African broadcast, they asked, "What is your key lesson, or the key thing you enjoy the most?" -- because it was a huge privilege to be part of such a project. The lesson from that was that it was Africa -- an African story -- that was used to share news with the rest of the world of what the benchmark can be for corporate turnarounds. Africa was being used as a success story!

So, I want to share with you a personal story about a turnaround or a transformation. And that has to do with me because in 1994, I packed a few things into a backpack and headed off for a year of travel in the middle of my university career. You should have seen my parents' reaction!

But very soon, I found myself from the southern part of Africa, in South Africa -- at the very north, in Egypt. And I sought out the most remote places. I went to the Siwa Oasis. That was one of my stops. And the Siwa Oasis is famous for several things, but the key thing is that it was the place that Alexander the Great went to when he wanted to find out what his destiny had in store for him. And legend has it that Alexander trekked through this desert. Half his battalion was wiped out in the sandstorm. And myth says that he had an audience with the oracle, and it foretold his destiny of greatness. This was 300 BC. So, Africa had long been seen as a place to go to for answers.

Now, the thing I remember about Siwa was the magical view of the sky at night. With no natural light source, Siva is one of these amazing places that when you look up you see a perfect tapestry. Fast forward to 2002. I'm sitting in Cambridge, Massachusetts at the Healthcare Development Conference. And I see the same picture, but from the opposite side. A satellite picture looking down at the earth. And it was that picture that made such a profound impact on me because I'll never forget it. I remember the very moment. And I wanted to share that image with you of what I saw at that point. The first thing that I saw was North America at night -- glowing, in all its glory. A warm feeling. Light.

And then I saw it -- Africa. Quite literally the "Dark Continent." And while Africa may be dark, the thing that brought the message home to me was that this is the challenge we are facing, but it's also the opportunity. Because whilst Africa may be dark -- other than the few specks that exist north and in the south and other areas -- it's aglow with the light in the hearts of the millions of people that are there. Entrepreneurs, dynamic people, people with hope. It was George Kimble, the geographer, who said that, "The only thing dark about Africa is our ignorance of it." So, let's start shedding light on this amazing eclectic continent that has so much to offer.

Let's start unpacking it. Africa is the second-largest continent, a landmass second from Asia. It also is the second most populated continent, with 900 million people. In fact -- coming back to the land mass -- Africa is so big that you could fit in the continental United States, China, and the entire Europe into Africa, and still have space. Africa is home to over 1,000 languages -- 2,000 is another estimate that's out there -- with over 2,000 languages and dialects. But you could say, "Invest in Africa in over 1,000 languages, and it wouldn't make a difference." What does the data say? As an investment banker, I'm in the cross-flow of information and the changes that are taking place in capital markets. So, I want to share with you some of these bellwether signals, or signs, and winds of change that are sweeping this continent.

So, let's start on that. And let's start at the high level, on the macro-factors. Inflation, in general, is coming down across Africa -- that's the first sign -- in many countries reaching double-digit figures. So, let's start looking at some of those. I call it my Z.E.N. cluster. Zambia: from 2004 to 2006, moves from the 18 percent in inflation to the nine percent. Egypt: from the 16 percent to about 8.4 percent. Nigeria: a similar situation, from the 16 percent to the eight percent. Single digits. More fascinating, you have other countries -- South Africa, Mauritius, Namibia -- all in single digits. But that's just part of the story. You have a similar trend with currencies going through an extreme time of stability. But that's looking at the big picture. And the first myth to dispel is that Africa is not a country.

It's made up of 53 different countries. So, the very definition -- to say "invest in Africa" is a no-go. It's meaningless. Each country has a unique value proposition. You can make money; you can lose money in Africa. But opportunities, boy oh boy, they exist. And this is what today is about -- it's about discussing those very opportunities. So, let's start getting into the countries and into the specific material and data. I was recently elected, as Emeka mentioned, as the President of the South

African Chamber of Commerce in America. And I'm very proud and happy to be in that role because it is a fascinating position to be in. To hear this dialogue that's just increasing in tenor and velocity, of decisions about trade and companies wanting to come. So, the first port of call: let's talk a little bit about South Africa. But not the South Africa we always talk about -- the gold, the minerals, the First World infrastructure -- a bit about the other side of it.

For example, South Africa was recently voted as the top destination for the top 1,000 UK companies for offshore call-centers. Same language, timeline, et cetera. Makes sense. Other headlines that have recently reached South Africa were Bain Capital and KKR, the big boys of private equity. Headline in South Africa: "They have landed." Quite ominous. But what were they there for? To acquire assets. Bing Capital's acquisition of Edcon, a large retailer, is testimony to the confidence they are starting to place in the economy. Because it is actually a long-term play. Being a retailer, it is a play on the belief that this middle-class that's growing will continue to grow, that the boom and the confidence in consumer spending will continue. But the story of Africa, and my focus, is beyond South Africa because there's so much happening. Undoubtedly, Nigeria is clearly a hot spot. Challenges -- and we will hear a lot about Nigeria in these four days.

But looking at Goldman Sachs' work -- we had the famous BRIC Report. The new report, "The Next Eleven," highlights that by 2020 Nigeria is going to be amongst the top 10 economies in the world. It's an investment opportunity. Think about that. Is anyone -- our banks, our investors -- seriously thinking about going to Nigeria? If you haven't, why not? What's going on in Nigeria? A couple of things. I want to talk about it from the perspective of capital markets. Bellwether signs again. Guarantee Trust Bank recently issued the first Euro Bond out of Africa, and this excludes South Africa. But the first Eurobond, the raising of international capital offshore, off its own balance sheet, without any sovereign backing -- that is an indication of the confidence that is taking place in that economy. Without any sovereign backing, a

Nigerian company raising capital offshore. It's just a sign of things to come.

Looking at the oil industry, Africa provides 18 percent of the U.S.'s oil supply, with the Middle East just 16 percent. It's an important strategic partner. Let's put Nigeria in perspective. 2.2 to 2.4 million barrels of oil a day -- the same league as Kuwait, the same league as Venezuela. But with Africa, let's start being careful about this. And Emeka and I have had these discussions. We have to move away from what's called "the curse of the commodities." Because it's not about oil, it's not about commodities. For Africa to truly be sustainable, we have to move beyond to other industries.

So, let's unpack those very quickly, and I'm going to move through these very, very, very fast because I can see that clock counting down. What else is going on there? Egypt. Egypt is launching a first large industrial zone -- 2.8 billion investment. The announcement just came out the last few weeks. Close to the Mediterranean, near Alexandria -- textiles, petrochemicals. It's being managed by a Singaporean-based management company. So they want to emerge as an industrial powerhouse across the industries -- away from oil.

Let's look at agriculture. Let's look at forestry. What's going on there? In Tanzania last week, we had the launch of the East African Organic Produce Standard. Again, gathering together farmers, gathering together stakeholders in East Africa to get standards for organic produce. Better prices. It ties in with small-scale farmers in terms of no pesticides, no fertilizers. Again, opportunity to tackle markets to get that higher price. Uganda: the New Forest Company, replanting and redeveloping their forests. Why is that important? As the energy needs are met and electricity is needed [we will need] poles for rolling out electricity. But here is the sweetener in the deal. They're going to be tapping into carbon credits. Let's go back to Nigeria. The banking sector has undergone tremendous transformation, from over 80 banks to 25 banks. Strengthening of the system. But what's going on there? Only 10 percent of the country is banked. The largest population in Africa is in Nigeria. 135 million-plus people. Think about that. There are only 700 ATMs in the country. Opportunity.

The same for telecoms across the country. Now let's look at the continent as a whole. People look at the roads, for example, and they'd say, "Angola: 90 percent of roads are untarred. Ah, problem!" It's more expensive to transport goods. Prices of goods go up, inflation is affected. Nigeria: 70 percent of roads are untarred. Zambia: 80 percent. In general, more than 50 percent of roads are untarred. This is an opportunity! Energy needs -- it's an opportunity. So what are the signs that things are fundamentally changing? Let's look at the stock markets in Africa. If I had to ask you, "In 2005 what was the best performing stock market or stock exchange in the world?" Would Egypt come to mind? In 2005, the Egyptian stock exchange returned over 145 percent. What's going on in some of the other countries? Let's look at some 2006 numbers. Kenya: over 60 percent. Nigeria: over 40 percent. South Africa: in the 20 percent. High ones. These are the trends that are taking place. But in any investment decision, the key question is, "What is my alternative investment?"

Because in Africa today, we are competing globally for capital. And global capital is agnostic -- it has no loyalties. There's an overhang of capital in the U.S., and the key is yield pickup. What Africa is providing is a diversification play, and also opportunities for yield pickup for the investor that's aware of what he or she is doing. Now, when looking at Africa vis-a-vis other things, and countries in Africa vis-a-vis other things, comparisons become important. 10 years ago, there, were very few countries that received sovereign ratings from the Standard & Poor's, Moody's and Fitch's. Today, 16 African countries and growing have sovereign country ratings. What does this mean? Take Nigeria again: double B-minus -- in the league of Ukraine and Turkey. Immediately we have a comparison. The backbone of making investment decisions for global holders of capital. Some other figures. South Africa: triple B-plus. Botswana: A-plus. Bakino Faso: B-minus. And so on.

In fact, one of the big agencies is setting up an office in Africa. Why are they doing that? Because they expect investment to follow. So, one of the big bellwethers, and one of my final points I want to mention, is the interesting thing I read is that CNBC has launched their first African channel. Why is CNBC doing this? It's the 24-hour rolling African news channel. They're doing it because they are expecting things to happen. Me and you, the investments we are going to be making, the investments the world is going to be making -- that's the 24-hour news channel dedicated to Africa. So that's the change that's coming down the pipeline.

So, in conclusion, I want to turn back to that very slide that made such a deep impact on me all those years ago. This time [I'll] give you the entire picture that I saw in 2002, and ask you that when you think about what your role can be in Africa, think about your journey in terms of bringing light to this continent. Because there are amazing opportunities available. And think about the concept of transformation in the back of your mind because things can be turned around rather quickly.

In 1899, Joseph Conrad released "The Heart of Darkness," a tale of grim horror along the Congo River. If one looks carefully, on the Congo River is one of those bright lights. And that's the very Congo river generating light -- the old heart of darkness now generating light with hydro-electric power. That is a transformation in power of ideas. So, the next step, over the next four days, is us exploring more of these ideas. And perchance, if you can always keep this picture in your mind, that when we convene maybe in the distant future, in 2020, that picture will look very different.

Chapter 8 Invest in Africa [1]

I want to start with a story, a la Seth Godin, from when I was 12 years old. My uncle Ed gave me a beautiful blue sweater -- at least I thought it was beautiful. And it had fuzzy zebras walking across the stomach, and Mount Kilimanjaro and Mount Meru were kind of right across the chest, that were also fuzzy. And I wore it whenever I could, thinking it was the most fabulous thing I owned.

Until one day in ninth grade, when I was standing with a number of the football players. And my body had clearly changed, and Matt, who was undeniably my nemesis in high school, said in a booming voice that we no longer had to go far away to go on ski trips, but we could all ski on Mount Novogratz. And I was so humiliated and mortified that I immediately ran home to my mother and chastised her forever letting me wear the hideous sweater. We drove to the Goodwill and we threw the sweater away somewhat

---

[1] Jacqueline Novogratz: founder and CEO of Acumen

ceremoniously, my idea being that I would never have to think about the sweater nor see it ever again.

Fast forward -- 11 years later, I'm a 25-year-old kid. I'm working in Kigali, Rwanda, jogging through the steep slopes, when I see, 10 feet in front of me, a little boy -- 11 years old -- running toward me, wearing my sweater. And I'm thinking, no, this is not possible. But so, curious, I run up to the child -- of course scaring the living bejesus out of him -- grab him by the collar, turn it over, and there is my name written on the collar of this sweater.

I tell that story, because it has served and continues to serve as a metaphor to me about the level of connectedness that we all have on this Earth. We so often don't realize what our action and our inaction do to people we think we will never see and never know. I also tell it because it tells a larger contextual story of what aid is and can be. That this traveled into the Goodwill in Virginia, and moved its way into the larger industry, which at that point was giving millions of tons of secondhand clothing to Africa and Asia. Which was a very good thing, providing low cost clothing. And at the same time, certainly in Rwanda, it destroyed the local retailing industry. Not to say that it shouldn't have, but that we have to get better at answering the questions that need to be considered when we think about consequences and responses.

So, I'm going to stick in Rwanda, circa 1985, 1986, where I was doing two things. I had started a bakery with 20 unwed mothers. We were called the "Bad News Bears," and our notion was we were going to corner the snack food business in Kigali, which was not hard because there were no snacks before us. And because we had a good business model, we actually did it, and I watched these women transform on a micro-level. But at the same time, I started a micro-finance bank, and tomorrow Iqbal Quadir is going to talk about Grameen, which is the grandfather of all micro-finance banks, which now is a worldwide movement -- you talk about a meme -- but then it was quite new, especially in an economy that was moving from barter into trade.

We got a lot of things right. We focused on a business model; we insisted on skin in the game. The women made their own decisions at the end of the day as to how they would use this access to credit to build their little businesses, earn more income so they could take care of their families better.

What we didn't understand, what was happening all around us, with the confluence of fear, ethnic strife and certainly an aid game, if you will, that was playing into this invisible but certainly palpable movement inside Rwanda, that at that time, 30 percent of the budget was all foreign aid. The genocide happened in 1994, seven years after these women all worked together to build this dream. And the good news was that the institution, the banking institution, lasted. In fact, it became the largest rehabilitation lender in the country. The bakery was completely wiped out, but the lessons for me were that accountability counts -- got to build things with people on the ground, using business models where, as Steven Levitt would say, the incentives matter. Understand, however complex we may be, incentives matter.

So when Chris raised to me how wonderful everything that was happening in the world, that we were seeing a shift in zeitgeist, on the one hand I absolutely agree with him, and I was so thrilled to see what happened with the G8 -- that the world, because of people like Tony Blair and Bono and Bob Geldof -- the world is talking about global poverty; the world is talking about Africa in ways I have never seen in my life. It's thrilling. And at the same time, what keeps me up at night is a fear that we'll look at the victories of the G8 -- 50 billion dollars in increased aid to Africa, 40 billion in reduced debt -- as the victory, as more than chapter one, as our moral absolution.

And in fact, what we need to do is see that as chapter one, celebrate it, close it, and recognize that we need a chapter two that is all about execution, all about the how-to. And if you remember one thing from what I want to talk about today, it's that the only way to end poverty, to make it history, is to build viable systems on the ground that deliver critical and affordable goods and services to the poor, in ways that are financially sustainable and scalable. If we do that, we really can make poverty history.

And it was that -- that whole philosophy -- that encouraged me to start my current endeavor called "Acumen Fund," which is trying to build some mini-blueprints for how we might do that in water, health and housing in Pakistan, India, Kenya, Tanzania and Egypt. And I want to talk a little bit about that, and some of the examples, so you can see what it is that we're doing. But before I do this -- and this is another one of my pet peeves -- I want to talk a little bit about who the poor are. Because we too often talk about them as these strong, huge masses of people yearning to be free, when in fact, it's quite an amazing story. On a macro level, four billion people on Earth make less than four dollars a day.

That's who we talk about when we think about "the poor." If you aggregate it, it's the third largest economy on Earth, and yet most of these people go invisible. Where we typically work, there's people making between one and three dollars a day. Who are these people? They are farmers and factory workers. They work in government offices. They're drivers. They are domestics. They typically pay for critical goods and services like water, like healthcare, like housing, and they pay 30 to 40 times what their middleclass counterparts pay -- certainly where we work in Karachi and Nairobi. The poor also are willing to make, and do make, smart decisions, if you give them that opportunity.

So, two examples. One is in India, where there are 240 million farmers, most of whom make less than two dollars a day. Where we work in Aurangabad, the land is extraordinarily parched. You see people on average making 60 cents to a dollar. This guy in pink is a social entrepreneur named Ami Tabar. What he did was see what was happening in Israel, larger approaches, and figure out how to do a drip irrigation, which is a way of bringing water directly to the plant stock. But previously it's only been created for large-scale farms, so Ami Tabar took this and modularized it down to an eighth of an acre. A couple of principles: build small. Make it infinitely expandable and affordable to the poor.

This family, Sarita and her husband, bought a 15-dollar unit when they were living in a -- literally a three-walled lean-to with a corrugated iron roof. After one harvest, they had increased their income enough to buy a second system to do their full quarter-acre. A couple of years later, I meet them. They now make four dollars a day, which is pretty much middle class for India, and they showed me the concrete foundation they had just laid to build their house. And I swear, you could see the future in that woman's eyes. Something I truly believe.

You can't talk about poverty today without talking about malaria bed nets, and I again give Jeffrey Sachs of Harvard huge kudos for bringing to the world this notion of his rage -- for five dollars you can save a life. Malaria is a disease that kills one to three million people a year. 300 to 500 million cases are reported. It's estimated that Africa loses about 13 billion dollars a year to the disease. Five dollars can save a life. We can send people to the moon; we can see if there's life on Mars -- why can't we get five-dollar nets to 500 million people?

The question, though, is not "Why can't we?" The question is how can we help Africans do this for themselves? A lot of hurdles. One: production is too low. Two: price is too high. Three: this is a good road in -- right near where our factory is located. Distribution is a nightmare, but not impossible. We started by making a 350,000-dollar loan to the largest traditional bed net manufacturer in Africa so that they could transfer technology from Japan and build these long-lasting, five-year nets. Here are just some pictures of the factory.

Today, three years later, the company has employed another thousand women. It contributes about 600,000 dollars in wages to the economy of Tanzania. It's the largest company in Tanzania. The throughput rate right now is 1.5 million nets, three million by the end of the year. We hope to have seven million at the end of next year. So, the production side is working. On the distribution side, though, as a world, we have a lot of work to do. Right now, 95 percent of these nets are being bought by the U.N., and then given primarily to people around Africa. We're looking at building on some of the most precious resources of Africa: people. Their women.

And so, I want you to meet Jacqueline, my namesake, 21 years old. If she were born anywhere else but Tanzania, I'm telling you, she could run Wall Street. She runs two of the lines, and has already saved enough money to put a down payment on her house. She makes about two dollars a day, is creating an education fund, and told me she is not marrying nor having children until these things are completed. And so, when I told her about our idea -- that maybe we could take a Tupperware model from the United States, and find a way for the women themselves to go out and sell these nets to others -- she quickly started calculating what she herself could make and signed up.

We took a lesson from IDEO, one of our favorite companies, and quickly did a prototyping on this, and took Jacqueline into the area where she lives. She brought 10 of the women with whom she interacts together to see if she could sell these nets, five dollars apiece, despite the fact that people say nobody will buy one, and we learned a lot about how you sell things. Not coming in with our own notions, because she didn't even talk about malaria until the very end. First, she talked about comfort, status, beauty. These nets, she said, you put them on the floor, bugs leave your house. Children can sleep through the night; the house looks beautiful; you hang them in the window. And we've started making curtains, and not only is it beautiful, but people can see status -- that you care about your children. Only then did she talk about saving your children's lives. A lot of lessons to be learned in terms of how we sell goods and services to the poor.

I want to end just by saying that there's enormous opportunity to make poverty history. To do it right, we have to build business models that matter, that are scalable and that work with Africans, Indians, people all over the developing world who fit in this category, to do it themselves. Because at the end of the day, it's about engagement. It's about understanding that people really don't want handouts, that they want to make their own decisions; they want to solve their own problems; and that by engaging with them, not only do we create much more dignity for them, but for us as well. And so I urge all of you to think next time as to how to engage with this notion and this opportunity that we all have -- to make poverty history -- by really becoming part of the process and moving away from an us-and-them world, and realizing that it's about all of us, and the kind of world that we, together, want to live in and share.

Roshdy Ebrahim

Chapter 9 A vehicle built in Africa, for Africa [1]

Since over 90 percent of passenger cars are imported, often used, they're just not designed for local usage. High import duties often compound the problem, sometimes doubling the price of a car. So most vehicles are either too expensive or too unreliable for the average consumer. Well-designed vehicles are only part of the transport challenge, though. For every 100 adults in Africa, less than five people actually own a vehicle. Public transport is available, and in countries like Kenya, it's often run by local entrepreneurs using minivans like this. But in most rural and peri-urban areas, it's fragmented and unreliable. In more remote areas without transport, people have to walk, typically tens of kilometers, to get to school or collect clean drinking water or buy supplies from nearby markets. Bad roads, disparate communities, low average income levels and inadequate vehicles all impair the transport system and ultimately constrain economic output.

)[1] Joel Jackson: founder and CEO of mobius motors

Despite this constraint, the Pan-African economy is booming. Combined GDP is already over two trillion dollars. This is a massive commercial and social opportunity, not a helpless continent. So why isn't there already something better? Around the world, automotive is quarter the manufacturing sector. But in Africa, it's generally been overlooked by carmakers, who are focused on larger, established markets and emerging economies like India and China. This lack of industrialization, which itself creates a vicious-cycle barrier to the emergence of industry, has caused the dependence on imports. There is a supply-demand disconnect, with the vast majority of automotive spending on the continent today, essentially funding an international network of car exporters instead of fueling the growth of local industry.

It's entirely possible to solve this disconnect, though, starting with products that people actually want. And this is what motivated me to start Mobius, to build a vehicle in Africa, for Africa. To us, this meant reimagining the car around the needs of the consumer, simplifying nonessential features like interior fixtures and investing in performance-critical systems like suspension to create durable and affordable vehicles built for purpose.

And built for purpose is exactly where we started with our first-generation model, Mobius II, which was designed as a really rugged, low-cost SUV, able to handle heavy loads and rough terrain reliably. This launched in 2015, and we've now developed the next-generation version based on customer feedback. For high stress and heavy loading, we engineered a sturdy steel space frame. To handle acute vibration from rough roads, we ruggedized the suspension. For potholes and uneven terrain, high ground clearance was a no-brainer. And to make this something customers could actually be proud to drive in, we designed an aspirational body aesthetic. Underpinning all of this, we simplified or eliminated components like parking sensors and automatic windows wherever we could, to keep costs low and sell this at half the price of a five-year-old SUV in Kenya today.

The new Mobius II launches in 2018. And while durable, affordable vehicles like this are vital, a broader solution to immobility needs to go further.

Over the last decade, a transport-centric, shared economy has connected people across Africa with minivans, auto rickshaws and sedans. It's just not operated very effectively or efficiently. Enabling better access to transport is all about strengthening this public transit network, empowering local entrepreneurs who already offer similar services in their communities to operate these services more profitably and more widely. With this aim, we're taking human-centered design a step further and developing a transport platform model, which enables owners to plug in different modules, like a goods cage or ambulance unit, and run other services like goods delivery or medical transport, as well as public transport. Transportation services like this are the fundamental driver of logistics, trade, social services, access to education, health care and employment. The transportation grid to physical economies is akin to the internet to virtual economies. And the impact of increased mobility is only part of the potential here.

Since the late 1700s, the Industrial Revolution has catapulted the development of economies around the world into thriving societies. Today, manufacturing is still the engine of economic growth and stability, even as new technologies have inevitably transformed the way we live. Making stuff is important, especially for nation-states wanting to boost employment, increase skills and reduce import dependence. But while few countries can skip this industrialized stage, many have negligible manufacturing output. There are various reasons for this, but one reason is universal: hardware is hard.

So, what are the challenges to industry, and how are we approaching them? The first issue many people think of is a lack of skilled labor. In areas where access to good primary and secondary education are limited and employment opportunities are scarce, a small skill base is inevitable. But that doesn't mean it's immutable. There's an abundance of smart, hardworking and ambitious people in Africa, obviously. What's really lacking are good jobs that offer a path not just to employment but also professional growth. The first person we employed at Mobius over six years ago was a mechanic named Kazungu. Kazungu had gone to school up to the age of 18 and worked as an odd-job mechanic. Joining the company at the time was a near-vertical learning curve. But he rose to the challenge, and with more technical guidance from an expanding engineering team, he's grown over the years to lead a group of mechanics in R&D prototyping. A thirst for learning and the work ethic to step up to a challenge are values we now recruit on. Pairing innate values like this with on-the-job training and systems has strengthened our skill base. This works really well on the production line, where work can be systematized around clear procedural instructions and then reinforced through training. In our experience, it is possible to build a skilled workforce, and we plan to hire hundreds more people using this approach.

A second challenge is a lack of suppliers. In countries like Kenya, there are only a handful of automotive suppliers manufacturing parts like electrical harnesses, seats and glass. It's a burgeoning group, and without much demand from industry, most of these suppliers have no impetus to grow. We've worked hard with a few of them to develop the capacity to consistently manufacture components at the quality levels we need, like this supplier in Nairobi, who are helping to reduce the production cost of metal brackets and improve their ability to build conformant parts to our engineering drawings. Supply and development is standard practice in automotive globally, but it needs to be applied from the ground up with a vast majority of local suppliers to properly bolster the ecosystem. And as production volumes rise, these suppliers can employ more staff, invest in better equipment and continue to develop new manufacturing techniques to further increase output.

Building up skills and suppliers are not the only hurdles to local industrialization, but they're good examples of how we think about the challenge. You see, we're not just reimagining the car, we're reimagining our entire value chain. None of this has been easy, and we're only just getting started. But once African industry starts to scale, the potential is huge. Better products, costing less, built locally, together creating millions of jobs. Frugal innovation offers a path to economic acceleration across many industries, and the future of this continent depends on it.

The Africa 2.0 I believe in can apply locally relevant design and a commitment to solving its industrial challenges to create a more connected, more prosperous future, not just for the privileged few, but for everyone.

Chapter 10 Affordable and sustainable electricity in Africa [1]

So right now, nearly one billion people globally don't have access to electricity in their homes. And in sub-Saharan Africa, more than half of the population remain in the dark.

So, you probably all know this image from NASA. There's a name for this darkness. It's called "energy poverty," and it has massive implications for economic development and social well-being. One unique aspect of the energy poverty problem in sub-Saharan Africa -- and by the way, in this talk when I "energy," I mean "electricity" -- one thing that's unique about it is there isn't much legacy infrastructure already in place in many countries of the region. So, for example, according to 2015 data, the total installed electricity capacity in sub-Saharan Africa is only about 100 gigawatts. That's similar to that of the UK.

So, this actually presents a unique opportunity to build an energy system in the 21st

---

[1] Rose M.Mutiso: energy researcher

century almost from scratch. The question is: How do you do that? We could look back to the past and replicate the ways in which we've managed to bring stable, affordable electricity to a big part of the world's population. But we all know that that has some well-known terrible side effects, such as pollution and climate change, in addition to being costly and inefficient. With Africa's population set to quadruple by the end of the century, this is not a theoretical question. Africa needs a lot of energy, and it needs it fast, because its population is booming and its economy needs to develop.

So, for most countries, the general trajectory of electrification has been as follows. First, large-scale grid infrastructure is put in place, usually with significant public investment. That infrastructure then powers productive centers, such as factories, agricultural mechanization, commercial enterprises and the like. And this then stimulates economic growth, creating jobs, raising incomes and producing a virtuous cycle that helps more people afford more appliances, which then creates residential demand for electricity.

But in sub-Saharan Africa, despite decades of energy projects, we haven't really seen these benefits. The energy projects have often been characterized by waste, corruption and inefficiency; our rural electrification rates are really low, and our urban rates could be better; the reliability of our electricity is terrible; and we have some of the highest electricity prices in the whole world. And on top of all of this, we are now facing the impacts of the growing climate catastrophe head-on. So, Africa will need to find a different path.

And, as it turns out, we are now witnessing some pretty exciting disruption in the African energy space. This new path is called off-grid solar, and it's enabled by cheap solar panels, advances in LED and battery technology, and combined with innovative business models. So, these off-grid solar products typically range from a single light to home system kits that can charge phones, power a television or run a fan.

I want to be clear: off-grid solar is a big deal in Africa. I have worked in the sector for years, and these products are enabling us to extend basic energy services to some of the world's poorest, raising their quality of life. This is a very good and a very important thing. However, off-grid solar will not solve energy poverty in Africa, and for that matter, neither will a top-down effort to connect every unserved household to the grid. See, I'm not here to rehash that played-out "on-versus-off-grid" or "old-versus-new" debate. Instead, I believe that our inability to grapple with and truly address energy poverty in Africa stems from three main sources.

First, we don't really have a clear understanding of what energy poverty is, or how deep it goes. Second, we are avoiding complex systemic issues and prefer quick fixes. And third, we are misdirecting concerns about climate change. Combined, these three mistakes are leading us to impose a Western debate on the future of energy and falling back on paternalistic attitudes towards Africa.

So, let me try and unpack these three questions. First, what exactly is energy poverty? The main energy poverty targeted indicator is enshrined in the UN's Seventh Sustainable Development Goal, or SDG 7. It calls for 100 percent of the world's population to have access to electricity by the year 2030. This binary threshold, however, ignores the quality, reliability or utility of the power, though indicators are currently being developed that will try and capture these things.

However, the question of when a household is considered "connected" is not quite clear-cut. So, for example, last year the Indian Prime Minister Narendra Modi declared all of the villages in India electrified, the criteria for electrification being a transformer in every village plus its public centers and 10 percent -- 10 percent -- of its households connected. Meanwhile, the International Energy Agency, which tracks progress against SDG 7, defines energy access as 50 kilowatt hours per person per year. That's enough to power some light bulbs and charge a phone, perhaps run a low-watt TV or fan for a few hours a day. Now, providing entry-level access is an important first step, but let's not romanticize the situation. By any standard, a few lights and not much else is still living in energy poverty. And what's more, these energy poverty indicators and targets cover only residential use. And yet, households account for just about one quarter of the world's electricity consumption. That's because most of our power is used in industries and for commerce.

Which brings me to my main point: countries cannot grow out of poverty without access to abundant, affordable and reliable electricity to power these productive centers, or what I call "Energy for Growth." As you can see from this graph, there's simply no such thing as a low-energy, high-income country. It doesn't exist. And yet, three billion people in the world currently live in countries without reliable, affordable electricity -- not just to power their homes but also their factories, their office buildings, their data centers and other economic activities. Merely electrifying households and microenterprises cannot solve this deeper energy poverty. To solve energy poverty, we need to deliver reliable, affordable electricity at scale, to power economy-wide job creation and income growth.

This need, however, bumps against an emerging narrative that, faced with climate change, we all need to transition from large, centralized power systems to small-scale distributed power. The growth of off-grid solar in Africa -- and let me repeat, off-grid solar is a good thing -- but that growth fits nicely into this narrative and has led to those claims that Africa is leapfrogging the old ways of energy and building its power system from the ground up, one solar panel at a time.

It's a nice, solicitous narrative, but also quite naïve. Like many narratives of technological disruption, often inspired by Silicon Valley, it takes for granted the existing systems that underpin all of this transformation. You see, when it comes to innovating and energy, the West is working around the edges of a system that is tried and tested. And so all the sexy stuff -- the rooftop solar, the smart household devices, the electric vehicles -- all of this is built on top of a massive and absolutely essential grid, which itself exists within a proven governance framework. Even the most advanced countries in the world don't have an example of an energy system that is all edges and no center at scale.

So ultimately, no approach -- be it centralized or distributed, renewable or fossil-based -- can succeed in solving energy poverty without finding a way to deliver reliable, affordable electricity to Africa's emerging industrial and commercial sectors. So, it's not just lights in every rural home. It's power for Africa's cities that are growing fast and increasingly full of young, capable people in desperate need of a job. This in turn will require significant interconnectivity and economies of scale, making a robust and modern grid a crucial piece of any energy poverty solution.

So, our second mistake is falling for the allure of the quick fix. You see, energy poverty exists within a complex socioeconomic and political context. And part of the appeal of new electrification models such as off-grid solar, for example, is they can often bypass the glacial pace and inefficiency of government. See, with small systems you can skip the bureaucracies and the utilities and sell directly to customers. But to confront energy poverty, you cannot ignore governments, you cannot ignore institutions, you cannot ignore the many players involved in making, moving and using electricity at scale, which is a way to say that when it comes to providing energy for growth, it's not just about innovating the technology, it's about the slow and hard work of improving governance, institutions and the broader macroenvironment.

OK, so this is all good and nice, you say. But what about climate change? How do we ensure a high-energy future for everyone while also curbing our emissions? Well, we'll have to make some complex tradeoffs, but I believe that a high-energy future for Africa is not mutually exclusive to a low-carbon future. And make no mistake: the world cannot expect Africa to remain in energy poverty because of climate change.

Actually, the facts show that the opposite is true. Energy will be essential for Africa to adapt to climate change and build resilience. You see, rising temperatures will mean increased demand for space cooling and cold storage. Declining water tables will mean increased pumped irrigation. And extreme weather and rising sea levels will require a significant expansion and reinforcement of our infrastructure. These are all energy-intensive activities. So balancing climate change and Africa's pressing need to transition to a high-energy future will be tough. But doing so is nonnegotiable; we will have to find a way. The first step is broadening the terms of the debate away from this either-or framing. And we also must stop romanticizing solutions that distract us from the core challenges.

And let's not also forget that Africa is endowed with vast natural resources, including significant renewable potential. For example, in Kenya, where I'm from, geothermal power accounts for half of our electricity generation, and with hydro being the other major source, we are already mainly powered by renewable energy. We also just brought online Africa's largest wind farm and East Africa's biggest solar facility.

In addition, new technology means that we can now run and design our power systems and use energy more efficiently than ever, doing more with less. Energy efficiency will be an important tool in the fight against climate change.

So, in closing, I'd just like to say that Africa is a real place with real people, navigating complex challenges and major transitions, just like any other region of the world.

And while each country and each region has its social, economic and political quirks, the physics of electricity are the same everywhere. And the energy needs of our economies are just as intensive as those of any other economy.

So, the expansion of household electrification through a mix of on- and off-grid solutions has had an incredible impact in Africa. But they are nowhere near sufficient for solving energy poverty. To solve energy poverty, we need generation of electricity from diverse sources at scale and modern grids to power a high-energy future, in which Africans can enjoy modern living standards and well-paying jobs. Africans deserve this, and with one of every four people in the world projected to be African by the year 2100, the planet needs it.

Chapter 11 Energy Africa between developing and fighting climate change [1]

Think about this. Californians use more electricity playing video games than the entire country of Senegal uses overall. Also, before gyms were shut down due to COVID, New Yorkers could work out in a 10-degree-Celsius gym because the cold apparently burns more calories. And yet only three percent of Nigerians have air conditioners.

As you can see, there's a mind-blowing gap between the energy haves and the energy have-nots. And across the globe, we have incredible energy inequality. Billions of people simply lack enough energy to build a better life: affordable, abundant and reliable energy to run their businesses without daily blackouts, to preserve their crops from rotting, to power lifesaving medical equipment, to work from home and do Zoom calls with their colleagues, to run trains and factories, basically, to grow and to prosper and to access both dignity and opportunity. Rich countries have that kind of

---

[1] Rose M.Mutiso: energy researcher

energy, whereas most countries in Africa, and many elsewhere simply don't. And those billions of people are falling further and further behind the rest of the world.

In addition to taking their energy abundance for granted, the wealthy take something else for granted: that everyone should fight climate change exactly the same way. Tackling climate change will require an accelerated transition to low-carbon energy sources. And yet, emissions continue to climb year after year, threatening to blow our tight carbon budget. That's what I want to talk about today.

The carbon budget is an estimation of the total emissions that our planet's atmosphere can safely absorb. Faced with an imperative to not explode this carbon budget, the world is looking at Africa in a completely contradictory way. On one side, it wants us to grow, to emerge from abject poverty, to build a middle class, to own cars and air conditioners and other modern amenities because after all, Africa is the next global market.

On the other side, because they are anxious to demonstrate action on climate change, rich countries in the West are increasingly restricting their funding to only renewable energy sources, effectively telling Africa and other poor nations to either develop with no carbon or to limit their development ambitions altogether.

Africa obviously needs to develop. That's non-negotiable. And I want to make the case today that Africa must be prioritized when it comes to what's left in the carbon budget. In other words, Africa must be allowed to, yes, produce more carbon in the short term so we can grow, while the rich world needs to drastically cut their emissions.

Africans have a right to aspire to the same prosperity that everyone else enjoys. And we deserve the same chance at a job, at an education, at dignity and opportunity. We also understand very well that the entire world needs to get to a zero-carbon future. This might sound contradictory, but consider these three points.

First, Africa isn't the culprit of climate change. It's a victim. Africa and its more than one billion people are among the most vulnerable to climate change on the planet, facing the worst impacts of extreme weather, drought and heat. And yet, if you look at the carbon footprint of the entire African continent, 48 African countries combined are responsible for less than one percent of accumulative carbon dioxide in the atmosphere. Even if every one of the one billion people in sub-Saharan Africa tripled their electricity consumption overnight, and if all of that new power came from natural gas-fired plants, we estimate that the additional CO_2 that Africa would add would equal to just one percent of total global emissions.

Second, Africa needs more energy to fight climate change, not less. Because of its climate vulnerability, Africa's climate fight is about adaptation and resilience, and climate adaptation is energy-intensive. To respond to extreme weather, Africans will need more resilient infrastructure. We're talking seawalls, highways, safe buildings and more. To cope with drought, Africans will need pumped irrigation for their agriculture, and many will need desalination for fresh water. And to survive soaring temperatures, Africans will need cold storage and ACs in hundreds of millions of homes, offices, warehouses, factories, data centers and the like. These are all energy-intensive activities. If we fail at mitigation, the rich countries' plan B for climate change is to simply adapt. Africans need and deserve that same capacity for adaptation.

Third, imposing mitigation on the world's poor is widening economic inequality. We're creating energy apartheid. Working in global energy and development, I often hear people say, "Because of climate, we just can't afford for everyone to live our lifestyles." That viewpoint is worse than patronizing. It's a form of racism, and it's creating a two-tier, global energy system with energy abundance for the rich and tiny solar lamps for Africans.

The global market for natural gas is a great example of this. Large Western companies are actively developing gas fields in African countries to run industry and generate electricity in

Asia or in Europe. And yet, when these same African countries want to build power plants at home to use gas for their own people, the Western development and finance communities say, "No, we won't fund that."

And here's the irony. Many poor countries are already far ahead of the West when it comes to transitioning to a low-carbon energy system. In Kenya, where I'm from, we generate most of our electricity carbon-free. Renewable sources such as geothermal, hydro and wind provide nearly 80 percent of our electricity. In the US, that figure is only 17 percent.

So, let me repeat my points. Everyone must get to a zero-carbon future. In the transition, Africa and other poor nations deserve to get the balance of what's remaining in the world's carbon budget. For economic competitiveness, for climate adaptation, for global stability and for economic justice, rich and high-emitting countries must uphold their responsibility to lead on decarbonization, starting in their own economies.

We all have a collective responsibility to turn the tide on climate change. If we fail, it won't be because Senegal or Kenya or Benin or Mali decided to build a handful of natural gas power plants to provide economic opportunity for their people.

Chapter 12 Crop insurance [1]

In Kenya, 1984 is known as the year of the cup, or the goro goro. The goro goro is a cup used to measure two kilograms of maize flower on the market, and the maize flower is used to make ugali, a polenta-like cake that is eaten together with vegetables. Both the maize and the vegetables are grown on most Kenyan farms, which means that most families can feed themselves from their own farm. One goro goro can feed three meals for an average family, and in 1984, the whole harvest could fit in one goro goro. It was and still is one of the worst droughts in living memory. Now today, I insure farmers against droughts like those in the year of the cup, or to be more specific, I insure the rains.

I come from a family of missionaries who built hospitals in Indonesia, and my father built a psychiatric hospital in Tanzania. This is me, age five, in front of that hospital. I don't think they thought I'd grow up to sell insurance. So, let me tell you how that happened.

---
[1] Rose Goslinga: micro insurer

In 2008, I was working for the Ministry of Agriculture of Rwanda, and my boss had just been promoted to become the minister. She launched an ambitious plan to start a green revolution in her country, and before we knew it, we were importing tons of fertilizer and seed and telling farmers how to apply that fertilizer and plant. A couple of weeks later, the International Monetary Fund visited us, and asked my minister, "Minister, it's great that you want to help farmers reach food security, but what if it doesn't rain?" My minister answered proudly and somewhat defiantly, "I am going to pray for rain." That ended the discussion. On the way back to the ministry in the car, she turned around to me and said, "Rose, you've always been interested in finance. Go find us some insurance."

It's been six years since, and last year I was fortunate enough to be part of a team that insured over 185,000 farmers in Kenya and Rwanda against drought. They owned an average of half an acre and paid on average two Euros in premium. It's microinsurance.

Now, traditional insurance doesn't work with two to three Euros of premium, because traditional insurance relies on farm visits. A farmer here in Germany would be visited for the start of the season, halfway through, and at the end, and again if there was a loss, to estimate the damages. For a small-scale farmer in the middle of Africa, the math's of doing those visits simply don't add up. So instead, we rely on technology and data. This satellite measures whether there were clouds or not, because think about it: If there are clouds, then you might have some rain, but if there are no clouds, then it's actually impossible for it to rain. These images show the onset of the rains this season in Kenya. You see that around March 6, the clouds move in and then disappear, and then around the March 11, the clouds really move in. That, and those clouds, were the onset of the rains this year. This satellite covers the whole of Africa and goes back as far as 1984, and that's important, because if you know how many times a place has had a drought in the last 30 years, you can make a pretty good estimate what the chances are of drought in the future, and that means that you can put a price tag on the risk of drought.

The data alone isn't enough. We devise agronomic algorithms which tell us how much rainfall a crop needs and when. For example, for maize at planting, you need to have two days of rain for farmers to plant, and then it needs to rain once every two weeks for the crop to properly germinate. After that, you need rain every three weeks for the crop to form its leaves, whereas at flowering, you need it to rain more frequently, about once every 10 days for the crop to form its cob. At the end of the season, you actually don't want it to rain, because rains then can damage the crop.

Devising such a cover is difficult, but it turned out the real challenge was selling insurance. We set ourselves a modest target of 500 farmers insured after our first season. After a couple of months' intense marketing, we had signed up the grand total of 185 farmers. I was disappointed and confounded. Everybody kept telling me that farmers wanted insurance, but our prime customers simply weren't buying. They were waiting to see what would happen, didn't trust insurance companies, or thought, "I've managed for so many years. Why would I buy insurance now?"

Now many of you know microcredit, the method of providing small loans to poor people pioneered by Muhammad Yunus, who won the Nobel Peace Prize for his work with the Grameen Bank. Turns out, selling microcredit isn't the same as selling insurance. For credit, a farmer needs to earn the trust of a bank, and if it succeeds, the bank will advance him money. That's an attractive proposition. For insurance, the farmer needs to trust the insurance company, and needs to advance the insurance company money. It's a very different value proposition. And so, the uptick of insurance has been slow, with so far only 4.4 percent of Africans taking up insurance in 2012, and half of that number is in one country, South Africa.

We tried for some years selling insurance directly to farmers, with very high marketing cost and very limited success. Then we realized that there were many organizations working with farmers: seed companies, microfinance institutions, mobile phone companies, government agencies. They were all providing loans to farmers, and often, just before they'd finalize the loan, the farmer would say, "But what if it doesn't rain? How do you expect me to repay my loan?" Many of these organizations were taking on the risk themselves, simply hoping that that year, the worst wouldn't happen. Most of the organizations, however, were limiting their growth in agriculture. They couldn't take on this kind of risk. These organizations became our customers, and when combining credit and insurance, interesting things can happen. Let me tell you one more story.

At the start of February 2012 in western Kenya, the rains started, and they started early, and when rains start early, farmers are encouraged, because it usually means that the season is going to be good. So they took out loans and planted. For the next three weeks, there wasn't a single drop of rain, and the crops that had germinated so well shriveled and died. We'd insured the loans of a microfinance institution that had provided those loans to about 6,000 farmers in that area, and we called them up and said, "Look, we know about the drought. We've got you. We'll give you 200,000 Euros at the end of the season." They said, "Wow, that's great, but that'll be late. Could you give us the money now? Then these farmers can still replant and can get a harvest this season." So, we convinced our insurance partners, and later that April, these farmers replanted. We took the idea of replanting to a seed company and convinced them to price the cost of insurance into every bag of seed, and in every bag, we packed a card that had a number on it, and when the farmers would open the card, they'd text in that number, and that number would actually help us to locate the farmer and allocate them to a satellite pixel. A satellite would then measure the rainfall for the next three weeks, and if it didn't rain, we'd replace their seed.

One of the first beneficiaries of this replanting guarantee was Bosco Mwinyi. We visited his farm later that August, and I saw the smile on his face when he showed us his harvest, because it warmed my heart and it made me realize why selling insurance can be a good thing. But you know, he insisted that we get his whole harvest in the picture, so we had to zoom out a lot. Insurance secured his harvest that season, and I believe that today, we have all the tools to enable African farmers to take control of their own destiny. No more years of the cup. Instead, I am looking forward to, at least somehow, the year of the insurance, or the year of the great harvest.

Chapter 13 Farming in Africa [1]

Since 1997, researchers at the University of Sussex have monitored global trends in armed conflict. Their research clearly shows that in Africa, over the last 10 years, armed conflict has gone up by sevenfold. Let's think about that: sevenfold in a single decade. Why is this?

We believe, as oxygen is to fire, so are unemployed youth to insecurity. We have a lot of youth on this continent. Youth like Sandra, who, on a Saturday morning in March 2014, woke up excited at the prospects of getting a coveted job at the Nigerian Immigration Services. She kissed her daughter goodbye, left her home, never to return. Sandra and 15 other young Nigerians died that day, applying for a job, in the ensuing stampede, as tens of thousands of people applied for a few thousand open positions.

In the last 20 years, 20 million youth have entered the Nigerian workforce alone. Today, half our population is under the age of 18. That's almost

---

)[1] kola Masha: agricultural leader

80 million people that will be entering the workforce in the next 20 years. My friends, if a wave of 20 million people entering the workforce triggered Niger Delta crisis, Fulani herdsmen crisis and Boko Haram, I ask you: What will four times that number do?

To do my part to solve this challenge, in 2012, I moved to a small village in northern Nigeria, in the center of the area most recently hit by the spread of insecurity, brutal bombings and searing poverty, with an idea: Could we create an economic buffer to halt the spread of this insecurity, by unlocking the power of agriculture as a job-creation engine?

We knew this had been done before in countries like Thailand, where, in 1980, they suffered from the same economic challenges as us. Today, however, Thailand produces two million cars a year -- more than the United Kingdom -- with over 30 percent of its workforce as highly commercial, profitable small farmers, with an unemployment rate of less than one percent. How did they do this? In the 80s, Thailand dramatically improved the productivity of its small farmers, ensuring that it was able to start to dominate export markets for produce. Building on this strength, they attracted investment and started to process, being able to export higher-value products like starch from cassava. Finally, coupled with investment in education, they started to expand to even higher-value manufacturing. To make our idea a reality and follow a path similar to Thailand, we knew that we would have to sell young farmers on farming.

A young man in northern Nigeria, for the purpose of today's discussion, we'll call "Saminu," made it very clear to me that this would not be easy. Saminu grew up in a beautiful village in northern Nigeria. And he tells wondrous stories of playing for hours with his friends, running up and down the beautiful rock formations that dot the countryside around his home. Despite this beauty, Saminu knew that the first chance he got, he would leave. He did not want to be a farmer. Growing up, he saw his parents work so hard as farmers, but barely get by. As he says, they had "babu" -- nothing.

Young farmers like Saminu do not have access to the cash to buy the farming products to pair with their hard work to be successful. When their meager harvest came in, desperate for cash, they would sell most of it at fire-sale prices, when, if they could just wait six months, they could get 50 percent more. Hence, Saminu left to the city, where he soon realized that life was not easy. He borrowed a very old motorcycle, with tires that were more patches than tires, to become a motorcycle taxi driver. He lived in constant fear every day that his precious, tattered motorcycle would be ripped away from him, as it had before. But he got it back, thankfully. He knew of others, however, who were not so lucky -- other young men who, once they'd lost their motorcycles, became destitute. Angry, these young men set out to wreak vengeance on a society that they believed had turned its back on them. Saminu told me that they joined insurgent groups, often acting as getaway drivers in bombings and kidnappings.

To end this cycle of insecurity, we must make farming a viable choice. We must ensure that these young men, on their small farms, can earn enough money to make a life for themselves; to make a future. The question now is how. Recognizing that Africa has grassroot-level leadership, we simply developed a model to bring the professional management and investment to scale to these grassroot leaders. We called it "Babban Gona" -- "great farm" in Hausa.

Upon reaching the village in 2012, I traveled from community to community, trying to convince people of our idea, trying to recruit farmer members. We failed woefully that first year, barely recruiting 100 brave souls. But we persevered. We kept doing what we promised, slowly we gained their trust. More farmers joined us. Fast-forward now five years. With a passionate and committed team and the tremendous support of our partners, we grew dramatically, today, serving 20,000 small farmers, enabling them to double their yields and triple their net income relative to their peers. We are very proud of the fact Fast-forward three years, Saminu has earned enough money to buy three goats for his mother to start a goat-rearing business, owns his own retail store and bought not one, but two motorcycles, with vanity license plates: "Babban Gona."

My friends, in the next 20 years, over 400 million Saminus are entering the African workforce, with potentially half of them having opportunities in agriculture. To unlock these opportunities, through models similar to ours, they would require 150 billion dollars a year in financing. This is a big number. But if we can tap into commercial debt, it is a small number -- only 0.1 percent of all the debt in the world today, 10 cents out of every 100 dollars. This is why we designed our model to be very different from conventional agricultural development programs. In a few short years, we have shown that our model works, is high-impact and can turn a profit, attracting commercial investors that do not typically invest in small farmers in Africa.

Imagine a world where millions of young men across Africa, hardworking young men, have other options. I know these driven, ambitious young men will make the right choice. We can realize this dream if they have a choice.

Chapter 14 How quinoa can help combat hunger and malnutrition [1]

Like so many of you, when I'm hungry, I open the fridge and get myself something to eat any time I want. This is something most of us who live in a developed country don't think much about.

However, it is a luxury that I didn't think I would ever have in my life when I lived in a refugee camp in Tanzania 23 years ago, or even seven years ago, when I was living in my home country of Rwanda before I moved to the USA.

I was only seven years old when my home country of Rwanda went through the tragedy of the genocide that took so many lives, and they made us flee the country, and we became refugees. Life in a refugee camp -- it wasn't life. It was survival. I saw a lot of people dying from disease, poor sanitation, hunger. Food became a rare commodity. There were bad days. My family and I would survive on the leaves and grasses from the forest. There were also worse times, when we

---

)[1] Cedric Habiyaremye: crop scientist, agricultural entrepreneur

would go two or three days without anything to eat at all, only drinking water from the swamp.

After three years in a refugee camp, we decided to return back to Rwanda. And our struggle with food continued. However, farming proved to be the only reliable source of food. But our food lacked the nutritional diversity, and we continued to depend on food assistance from the United Nations World Food Program to balance our diet.

Still today, more than 70 percent of Rwandans, they work in the agriculture sector. But malnutrition and stunting remain rampant. I came to realize that food insecurity and malnutrition were not happening because people were not farming enough; it was because people were not farming the right crops.

I eventually left Rwanda and moved to the USA for graduate school and discovered the possible solution to that problem. And that solution is quinoa.

Quinoa is indigenous to the Indian regions of South America, in countries like Bolivia, Peru ... And it's very well-known for its powerhouse nutrient, and the crop has all the nine essential amino acids, making it a complete protein. But unfortunately, quinoa is not cultivated as much in different parts of the world.

In Rwanda, for example, beans are the only thing that kept so many of us alive during those times of hunger and starvation. As a matter of fact, Rwanda is the number one beans-consuming country in the world per capita. In this part of Africa, beans are one of the only crops that provide immediate food source, because you can eat beans at every stage of growth. We eat beans, leaves and green beans before harvest. Unfortunately, you cannot cultivate beans in the same field season after season. You need to ensure there is regular rotation to avoid disease and pests.

Like beans, farmers can enjoy the nutritious quinoa leaves. While beans are considered nutritious, quinoa has far more micronutrients, and with quinoa, you can make many [more] different food products and drinks than beans. In 2015, alongside my research team at Washington State University, we introduced quinoa in Rwanda for the first time. We tested 20 varieties of quinoa to see the adaptability in three ecological zones of Rwanda. And the results were astonishing.

Among the 20 varieties we tested, 15 of them showed the potential to grow well in Rwanda's climate. And later, we started Quinoa Model Farmers Program. We gave those potential varieties to farmers to grow in their farm and community. We started with 12 farmers, and three years later, we are now working with around 500 farmers, including my mother, who is locally known as "the queen of quinoa" because of her work in helping other farmers adopt this crop.

We give them seeds, train them how to grow it and how to cook it. And farmers are pretty creative, coming up with recipes of their own. And we've started seeing remarkable changes in their lives, including success stories that many of them can now have access to nutritious food three times a day.

I'd like to note that quinoa is not meant to entirely [push out] other crops. We introduced quinoa as a supplement to create overall health and nutrition, rounding out diet to combat chronic malnutrition. We have started this model with quinoa in Rwanda, but it can be replicated in different countries experiencing hunger and malnutrition. About one in nine people in the world suffer from chronic malnutrition. We have started research collaboration with institutions in countries like Kenya, Malawi, Uganda and other countries experiencing hunger and malnutrition.

And quinoa isn't the only magic crop. There are several crops with high adaptability and nutritional value, crops like millet, sorghum, fonio, barley, oat, to name a few. These crops have high adaptability and respond well to climate change. You can grow these magic crops in different parts of the world, bridging the gap, so that there is accessible nutritious food for everyone.

I know how it feels to be hungry. I've been there. And I know how it feels to be malnourished, because I've been there, too. Introducing crops with high biodiversity, adaptability and nutritional value will play an important role in creating food security, seed sovereignty and sustainable production in communities and countries that are experiencing hunger and malnutrition.

Having nutritious food should not be a luxury. There is a need to ensure that there is accessible and affordable nutritious food for everyone. And this is a step towards making it a reality.

References

1. Andrew Mwenda: journalist
2. Cedric Habiyaremye: crop scientist, agricultural entrepreneur
3. Chika Ezeanya: Before We Set Sail, amazon– March 7, 2012
4. Euvin Naidoo: investment banker
5. G. Ayitta: Africa Unchained: The Blueprint for Africa's Future, amazon 2006
6. Jacqueline Novogratz: founder and CEO of Acumen
7. Joel Jackson: founder and CEO of mobius motors
8. kola Masha: agricultural leader
9. Robert Neuwirth: author
10. Rose Goslinga: micro insurer
11. Rose M.Mutiso: energy researcher
12. Sangu Delle: entrepreneur and clean water activist.
13. Wanjira Mathai: environmentalist, social entrepreneur, youth leadership advocate.

www.ingramcontent.com/pod-product-compliance
Lightning Source LLC
Chambersburg PA
CBHW060849220526
45466CB00003B/1297